ONE CREATIVE WRITING PROMPT A DAY

ONE
Creative
Writing
PROMPT
A DAY

A JOURNAL TO BUILD YOUR CRAFT AND UNLOCK YOUR INNER STORYTELLER

LITA KURTH

callisto publishing
an imprint of Sourcebooks

Copyright © 2024 by Callisto Publishing LLC

Cover and internal design © 2024 by Callisto Publishing LLC

Illustrations by iStock/Getty Images: © anna (pink backgrounds); © aleksandarvelasevic (frame)

Author photo courtesy of Julie Kitzenberger

Art Director: Lisa Schreiber

Art Producer: Stacey Stambaugh

Editor: Adrian Potts

Production Editor: Rachel Taenzler

Production Manager: Martin Worthington

Callisto and the colophon are registered trademarks of Callisto Publishing LLC.

Published by Callisto Publishing LLC C/O Sourcebooks LLC

P.O. Box 4410, Naperville, Illinois 60567-4410

(630) 961-3900

callistopublishing.com

Printed and bound in the United States of America.

SB 10 9 8 7 6 5 4 3 2 1

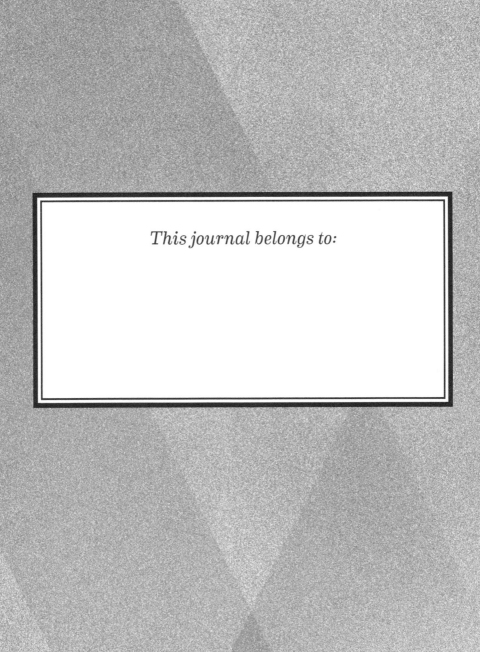

This journal belongs to:

Introduction

Dear Writer,

Yes, that's you. Perhaps you don't dare to use the word "writer" yet. Maybe you quake at the thought of coming out of the "writer's closet." I did too, once. Many pages, groups, classes, books, conferences, projects, and publications later, I claim the word "writer." And it all began with me, a notebook, and a hope.

If this is your first step into writing, welcome to a day-by-day practice that is a journey into the self and the world. As with any art, if you are devoted and having fun, you will surely progress.

Perhaps you've been writing for a while. You've undertaken a long project but you're stuck or bored. Or you can't think of a new writing project. As part of my writing practice, I often write to prompts. In the company of other people, I set a timer and off we go. It's amazing what you can write in fifteen minutes, given low stakes and a free spirit. Often that scrap of writing enlivens my current project or grows into a story.

There is no one right way to use this book. In this journal, you'll see that some prompts come in clusters. Others are solo. You may use these prompts to invite memory, incite poetry, or add to your novel.

Some of you will write first thing every morning. Good for you, if you can do that. Others might write to seven prompts during the one day they have free for writing. Some will start at the beginning and work steadily through. Others will browse until they find a prompt that strikes them. Others still will start at the end. Some will write alone. Others will write with friends, online or in person. Some will fill in the date. Others won't.

It's your writing journal. Do as the Muse commands. May you find this journal a source of enjoyment and freedom, a nudge to make the day more meaningful. You might end up with an artifact you want to keep, even pass down. Someday you may have dozens of these journals, as I do. But wherever your writing journey takes you—and I've found my journey both wondrous and unpredictable—please know that you go with my best wishes.

—*Lita Kurth*

Writing
Prompts

__ / __ / ____

Your writing journey begins today. Take a moment to imagine your Muse, that inexhaustible source of inspiration and creativity. Describe the Muse in detail. Then write a letter asking your Muse for assistance this year. Be as specific as you like.

_____

_____

_____

_____

_____

_____

_____

_____

_____

_____

_____

_____

_____

_____

_____

__ / __ / ____

List ten things your character is told by a bossy neighbor to do "for your own good."

_____

_____

_____

_____

_____

_____

_____

__ / __ / ____

List your character's replies to each of the bossy neighbor's admonitions.

_____

_____

_____

_____

_____

_____

_____

_____

_____

__ / __ / ____

Your main character lives above a florist in a small town. Have the character walk through the shop holding an important package that doesn't belong to them and that they want to keep hidden. Describe the scene, including physical details of the shop.

_____

_____

_____

_____

_____

_____

_____

_____

_____

_____

_____

_____

_____

_____

___ / ___ / ___

Look out a window. Describe in detail what you see, including size, color, what's near, and what's far. To what extent does it mirror your internal weather: How you feel at this moment? Now describe a character using some of these details, either contrasting or echoing their internal and external worlds.

_____

_____

_____

_____

_____

_____

_____

_____

_____

_____

_____

_____

_____

_____

_____

_____

_____

__ / __ / ____

A teen from a farming town goes to a psychic and learns that someone close to them is lying. Write the journal entry in which they try to guess who it is.

__ / __ / ____

Describe a zombie moving across a field. Use as many words as possible with long A sounds: shake, chase, stake, fate, gray, gaze, pale, and so on.

__ / __ / ____

Write about two Parisians fighting over an umbrella. Include the color turquoise and a gust of wind.

__ / __ / ____

Friendly dolphins join a person swimming in a Florida bay. Use the sense of touch to describe the swimmer's experience: arms, legs, trunk, and face.

___ / ___ / ___

Your character, a stockbroker, is worried about their job. Describe their visit to a tarot reader where the Nine of Swords appears, foretelling guilt, imprisonment, anxiety, suffering, and alienation. How does your character respond emotionally? What actions do they take?

_____

_____

_____

_____

_____

_____

_____

_____

_____

_____

_____

_____

_____

_____

___ / ___ / ____

Retell the story "Three Billy Goats Gruff" from the troll's point of view. (Look up the story online if you are unfamiliar with it.) How did the troll come to live under a bridge, for example? Describe his view of each goat that comes across his bridge.

_____

_____

_____

_____

_____

_____

_____

_____

_____

_____

_____

_____

_____

_____

_____

_____

_ / _ / ___

Your character, a spy on the planet Venus, discovers in a Zoom meeting that their "boss" is actually an imposter from their chief enemy, the Martians. Show your character trying to find out if a colleague knows. Include an irregular badge.

_____

_____

_____

_____

_____

_____

_ / _ / ___

Personify anger and describe how you feel when it is in charge. Begin with something like, "Anger drove me here. I hate his driving." Give details of exactly how anger behaves.

_____

_____

_____

_____

_____

_____

_____

__ / __ / ____

A new government in 2500 enlists your character as a time-travel emissary to make reparations for past crimes. They travel to the starving Northern Cheyenne tribe of Montana in 1877, bringing a truckload of goods. What do they bring and how do they arrange reparations?

_____

_____

_____

_____

_____

_____

_____

_____

_____

_____

_____

_____

_____

_____

_____

_____

__ / __ / ____

Your character wakes from sleepwalking to find themselves in a backyard of the Chicago suburbs. Describe the ordinary sounds they hear (water, animals, rustling leaves, and so on) and one unusual one.

__ / __ / ____

Two clouds float over a football game and comment on the action below. Show their disagreement over a foul.

__ / __ / ____

Your character describes an artwork (real or imagined) using very opinionated words. Have them comment on the objects in the artwork and the type of frame.

__ / __ / ____

Describe an apartment using as many words that begin with F as possible: fan, fleas, furnace, and so on. Notice the effect of these sounds on your prose.

__ / __ / ____

Write in first person (I) the life story of an abandoned pickup truck. Describe its color, size, type, interior, and perhaps the license plate. Then focus on the three most important events of its "life." Include how it ended up with specific dents and broken parts.

_____

_____

_____

_____

_____

_____

_____

_____

_____

_____

_____

_____

_____

_____

___ / ___ / _____

A person down on their luck buys a pitcher with a cow painted on it from a thrift store. The next day, a tiny cow appears in their apartment. Show your character discovering it and deciding what to do. Include smells and sounds.

_____

_____

_____

_____

_____

_____

___ / ___ / _____

Soon after, the person comes home to find the cow has doubled in size. Now what will they do? Show them brainstorming with a friend.

_____

_____

_____

_____

_____

_____

__ / __ / ____

Your character attends a service at a new religious center in town. Gradually, they realize this religion is dedicated to the University of Iowa women's basketball team. Describe the sermon, choir robes, and your character's impressions. Do they plan to return?

_____

_____

_____

_____

_____

_____

_____

_____

_____

_____

_____

_____

_____

__ / __ / ____

Describe your music-celebrity character's favorite T-shirt and a particular place they wore it.

__ / __ / ____

Your character is served their most hated breakfast cereal. Describe it in detail, including the sound.

__ / __ / ____

A poet envisions an epic project but struggles with self-doubt. However, they have a dream of reassurance. Describe the figures in the dream.

__ / __ / ____

Depressed and disconsolate, a parent sits wearily on a couch. Describe all the ways the family dog offers comfort as the parent tells the dog about their day.

__ / __ / ____

Your character attends a party where candles are burning in every room: next to curtains, next to a stack of newspapers, and next to cushions. Describe your character navigating the room and taking bold action with an unexpected result.

_____

_____

_____

_____

_____

_____

_____

_____

_____

_____

_____

_____

_____

_____

__ / __ / ____

Investigating a possible art counterfeiter, a detective visits them at home and pretends to be a reporter doing a story about art collectors. Describe the power struggle as the reporter attempts to photograph the counterfeiter in front of paintings and the counterfeiter attempts to redirect without creating suspicion.

___/___/____

Create a dialogue in which two friends disagree about whether a dog is attractive or not and who it is the reincarnation of. (They don't disagree that it's the reincarnation of someone.) Include details of the dog and the day it was acquired/adopted/found.

_____

_____

_____

_____

_____

_____

_____

_____

_____

_____

_____

_____

_____

_____

__ / __ / ____

A student meets an inspiring, though not famous, actor who has a very high opinion of themself. Write a scene at a bar where the actor calls themself a genius, comparable to Robert De Niro. Include specific drinks and a third character who is an eavesdropper.

_____

_____

_____

_____

_____

_____

__ / __ / ____

Begin a story that breaks a common rule about story-writing: Start with the trivia of getting out of bed, eating, brushing teeth, and so on. Make it as quirky, curiosity-inspiring, and dramatic as possible.

_____

_____

_____

_____

_____

_____

__ / __ / ____

An elevator gets stuck for three hours with a plumber, an architect, and a waiter inside. Each faces a problem: a desperate need for the bathroom, a child needing to be picked up, and a client waiting to sign a contract. Which problem goes with which character? How do they help one another?

_____

_____

_____

_____

_____

_____

_____

_____

_____

_____

_____

_____

_____

__ / __ / ____

Write a flash (short) story in which an old bathroom rug tries to ingratiate itself with a fancy new shower curtain, who at first ignores and then sharply rejects the rug. How does the rug get revenge? Make each voice distinctive.

_____

_____

_____

_____

_____

_____

_____

_____

_____

_____

_____

_____

_____

_____

_____

__ / __ / ____

An advertising executive receives a request for a billboard campaign for the security services of a Mafia don. Provide two or three possible slogans and describe the accompanying visuals.

_____

_____

_____

_____

_____

_____

__ / __ / ____

Two chickens receive a special treat of greenery they have never had before: miner's lettuce (look it up). Provide their ecstatic dialogue and over-the-top comparisons to their normal chicken feed.

_____

_____

_____

_____

_____

_____

_ / _ / ___

Write a piece titled "How to Lose Your Job." Include tools, setting, and personalities of a manager and coworkers at a fast-food job. Is it an unfair dismissal or well-earned?

_____

_____

_____

_____

_____

_____

_____

_____

_____

_____

_____

_____

_____

_____

___ / ___ / _____

Define an abstract word with two concrete examples. For example, compassion is the shirt taken off and pressed on the wound of an accident victim.

___ / ___ / _____

Add to the first example you wrote: a scent, a sound, a specific place, and two lines of dialogue.

___ / ___ / _____

Add to the second example: a scent, a sound, a specific place, and two lines of dialogue.

___ / ___ / _____

Add to the third example: a scent, a sound, a specific place, and two lines of dialogue.

__ / __ / ____

A family gathers on the moon for a ceremony involving flashlights to commemorate the day the parents immigrated. An argument arises between the generations about whether or not to return to Earth, which is extremely dangerous but filled with luxuries. Describe the scene, then show the argument.

__ / __ / ____

An accountant is in love with an interior designer. Show the accountant's response to the alluring words and actions of the designer as they work on a project together, but don't directly reveal the accountant's love.

_____

_____

_____

_____

_____

_____

_____

__ / __ / ____

Your character learns they have a half-sibling conceived when their parent lived in another country. All they have is a photo of the sibling. In the voice of your character, write a letter to that country's embassy asking for help locating the person. Describe the photo.

_____

_____

_____

_____

_____

_____

___ / ___ / ____

A manager keeps bringing in Swiss chard for their staff, but no one on staff likes Swiss chard. Describe a secretive meeting in which the staff discuss ways to stop further Swiss chard gifts.

__ / __ / ____

Describe what makes you (or your character) a Southern/Northern/Midwestern/
East Coast/West Coast writer. Include a regional shop, a crop, and a festival.

_____

_____

_____

_____

_____

_____

_____

_____

_____

_____

_____

_____

_____

_____

__ / __ / ____

An artist plans to honor their mentor with a work of art. Describe the proposed work.

__ / __ / ____

The artist assembles tools and supplies. Describe several of these. Include at least one smell.

__ / __ / ____

The artist works in secret in a cramped workspace. Describe the workspace.

__ / __ / ____

The mentor receives the work. Include a pleasant surprise and how the mentor's eyes appear.

___ / ___ / ___

Your character goes outside to see a neighbor (whom your character has never liked) letting their child pick all of the tulips in your character's front yard. Describe your character's attempts to be nice to the child yet save the flowers.

___/___/_____

Your character caught a five-foot alligator to eat for dinner, but it got away and hid somewhere in the house. Your character grabs a utensil and goes hunting. What utensil? Where does your character find the alligator? What happens?

_____

_____

_____

_____

_____

_____

___/___/_____

Write a dialogue between two peanuts in a shell who are awakened by someone shaking their shell. One has a positive interpretation of what's about to occur, and the other, a negative one.

_____

_____

_____

_____

_____

_____

Your character has the same name as a famous socialite. One day, they receive free tickets to a private box at the opera house. Your character rents a formal outfit and shows up at the private box. Describe what happens when the real socialite appears.

___ / ___ / _____

Choose an ordinary object you have at home—a clay pot, a pencil, a broom, or something else. Now write two or three short scenes (including a specific time, place, and event) that involve family members having a conflict over that item. (Fierce arguments over something trivial can create great comedy.)

__ / __ / ____

A political campaign staffer discovers a hidden microphone in the luxury condominium where a big political fundraiser is about to take place. List their options.

__ / __ / ____

Show the campaign staffer's words and actions as they cancel the party.

__ / __ / ____

As an alternate storyline, show the campaign staffer discreetly enlisting all the party guests to look for hidden microphones.

__ / __ / ____

Show the campaign staffer responding in another way (your choice).

Write a scene in which two siblings disagree about a piano. As soon as they reach a compromise, a third sibling comes in and threatens to undo the truce. Is the third sibling successful? Give each sibling a unique look and way of speaking.

__ / __ / ____

Begin a piece with these words: "This is how I ended up living with my ex-mother-in-law." Include a description of the ex-spouse, cheap coffee, and lawn mowing (done by the mother-in-law).

_____

_____

_____

_____

_____

_____

_____

_____

_____

_____

_____

_____

_____

_____

__/__/____

In a detailed list, offer five things a lizard is grateful for, ranked from minor to major.

__/__/____

Someone with an unusual hairdo and necklace enters a bar where your character is having a beer. Zero in on your character's critique of the stranger.

__/__/____

While stirring a pot, your character looks down and sees a face. What kind of face? What does it say?

__/__/____

Write a ship's log listing a series of bad occurrences, each worse than the last.

__ / __ / ____

Your character, a struggling actor, runs into an old acting-school friend on Park Avenue who says, "Don't speak to me unless it's to ask for an autograph." Describe the friend's fancy clothes, snooty voice, and gestures, as well as your character's response.

_____

_____

_____

_____

_____

_____

_____

_____

_____

_____

_____

_____

_____

_____

___ / ___ / ___

A butchered rooster comes back to haunt the farmer who chopped off his head.
Describe the rooster's three hauntings, each more startling than the previous.
Weave in the remaining chickens abetting the rooster ghost during each haunting.

_____

_____

_____

_____

_____

_____

_____

_____

_____

_____

_____

_____

_____

_____

_____

__ / __ / ____

In downtown Dallas, an attractive but naive out-of-towner drops a bag of Dollar Store purchases. A friendly passerby steps in to assist but makes things worse. Describe what they say and what happens.

_____

_____

_____

_____

_____

_____

_____

__ / __ / ____

A bottle of organic spinach juice finds itself put into a box of high-caffeine, extra-sugar soft drinks. Give the two kinds of beverages distinct accents as you describe the organic juice's efforts to fit in.

_____

_____

_____

_____

_____

_____

_____

__ / __ / ____

A lacquered wooden bowl painted with a scene of a turquoise sky and reddish sand takes your character's memory back to a night in the Tunisian desert when a Berber guide pointed out the constellations in the night sky. Write that scene. Try to capture a sense of awe and appreciation.

_____

_____

_____

_____

_____

_____

_____

_____

_____

_____

_____

_____

_____

_____

_____

___ / ___ / _____

Your character hates small talk, so one day they give outrageous answers to clerks and receptionists who chat with them. Sample question: "Got weekend plans?" Sample answer: "I'm going to chop down every tree in my neighborhood." What response makes your character stop?

__ / __ / ____

Your character, a nature photographer in Wisconsin, rises at dawn to photograph beaver dams. They discover a dead beaver and suspect foul play. A ranger comes by, and they discuss possible suspects. Using third-person narrative (she, he, they), write that scene.

_____

_____

_____

_____

_____

_____

__ / __ / ____

In their blog, the nature photographer shares photos, lays out their suspicions, and asks for help. Someone replies, but do they really want to help? Write both the blog post and the reply in first person (I).

_____

_____

_____

_____

_____

_____

__ / __ / ____

Your character, a flight instructor, reassures a nervous pilot trainee before takeoff. But in the middle of the flight, the engine conks out. Describe their interchange and your character's physical feelings as they make an emergency landing in a wheat field.

_____

_____

_____

_____

_____

_____

_____

_____

_____

_____

_____

_____

_____

_____

__ / __ / ____

In the year 2200, a detective discovers that someone has stolen an entire day from them. They jump into a time machine to seek the perpetrators. Show them finding evidence of the crime on a planet of criminals.

__ / __ / ____

Describe your character's life in a series of numbers (for example, 2nd of 10 children, 17 years of pickled herring and saunas, 8 years of woodsmoke and fast toboggans, and 2 years of numb toes and mosquitoes).

__ / __ / ____

Your character buys a magical calendar from a mysterious, old shopkeeper. The calendar propels your character into another year every lunch hour. Describe them explaining their sudden appearance in Sherwood Forest to Robin Hood.

_____

_____

_____

_____

_____

_____

_____

_____

_____

_____

_____

_____

_____

_____

__ / __ / ____

Give each of three hours a particular sound, smell, setting, and household item (for example, 8 a.m., oatmeal bubbling and steaming on the gas stove, smell of grain, rain lashing the window outside).

_____

_____

_____

_____

_____

_____

_____

__ / __ / ____

Describe a dining room and its furniture and who in the family sits where, including someone who is never there for meals but has a place set. What does the location of each seat say about the power of the person who occupies it?

_____

_____

_____

_____

_____

_____

_____

__ / __ / ____

Your character and their mate are traveling from Chicago to New Orleans when their van breaks down and they catch the flu. Show them coping with the worst day and growing closer in the process.

___ / ___ / _____

A bath towel falls in love with a washcloth, but the towel loves dryness and the washcloth loves wetness. Write a dialogue in which the towel proposes.

___ / ___ / _____

A hand towel enters and offers to facilitate the match. Show this happening and whether the offer is sincere.

___ / ___ / _____

Write the ending of the towel-washcloth love story as a tragedy.

___ / ___ / _____

Write the ending of the towel-washcloth love story as a comedy.

___ / ___ / _____

A struggling photographer gets up early to photograph thrushes. Focusing in on a photo, they notice a diamond ring on a thrush's leg. Describe the photographer's obsessive search for the ring. Are they successful in capturing the ring?

_____

_____

_____

_____

_____

_____

_____

_____

_____

_____

_____

_____

_____

An eighteenth-century seamstress secretly loves a gentleman and embroiders love words into the design on the handkerchiefs she sews for him. Describe one handkerchief in detail and the day she gives it to him. Does he notice the words? How does he react?

_____

_____

_____

_____

_____

_____

_____

_____

_____

_____

_____

_____

_____

_____

_____

_____

__ / __ / ____

Write a middle schooler's diary entry in which they rant about the slang, clothing, hairstyles, and music that are popular around them, which don't fit their view of the world or of themself. Include something about a yearbook and a song.

_____

_____

_____

_____

_____

_____

_____

_____

_____

_____

_____

_____

_____

_____

___ / ___ / _____

A high school student comes into their grandma's house on a hot afternoon to find the grandmother burning papers. When the grandmother leaves the room, the student grabs an unburned piece of paper and discovers . . . what?

_____

_____

_____

_____

_____

_____

___ / ___ / _____

Write about two friends from college who are now on divergent paths having a potentially friendship-ending conversation. Include a family business and an argument about words.

_____

_____

_____

_____

_____

_____

___ / ___ / _____

Your character's friend has changed their kitchen from lilac and white to bright red and yellow. Write your character's internal monologue as they walk through the new kitchen, viewing walls, ceiling, appliances, and artificial flowers. Their friend asks, "Do you like it?" End with your character's answer.

_____

_____

_____

_____

_____

_____

_____

_____

_____

_____

_____

_____

_____

__ / __ / ____

Write a story in which your character walks into a lake to drown, but a kind, friendly fisherperson nearby causes them to change their mind. They eat grilled fish with the fisherperson and take a new direction. Include smells, sounds, and sights.

___ / ___ / ____

Describe a particular pair of shoes your character had as a child and one important event that happened while they were wearing the shoes (a recital? an accident? a party?).

_____

_____

_____

_____

_____

_____

_____

___ / ___ / ____

Add the metacommentary (text in which the writer intrudes in the story) "Here's what I don't know" and continue the story.

_____

_____

_____

_____

_____

_____

_____

___ / ___ / _____

Your character appears at work during a national epidemic, unaware that on social media they've been accused of hoarding crucial medications. Write a scene describing their interactions with coworkers that gradually reveal this situation. Is your character actually guilty?

___ / ___ / _____

Your character explores a German city. Describe ten unique smells they encounter and their responses to them. Examples might be white lilacs on Mozart Street, car exhaust fumes, trees in a park, or the cherry, chocolate, and liqueur from a Black Forest cake.

_____

_____

_____

_____

_____

_____

_____

_____

_____

_____

_____

_____

_____

_____

_____

_____

_____

_____

_____

_____

__ / __ / ____

A violinist receives unexpected advice from an audience member. They respond with disordered music dedicated to that person. Describe the debut of that piece of music and the reaction of the audience member.

_____

_____

_____

_____

_____

_____

__ / __ / ____

A poet, unable to find an audience, goes to the beach and begins reciting a rousing poem to the fish. Many fish rise up and listen. Describe the types of fish and their comments. Are they impressed? Do they heckle? Both?

_____

_____

_____

_____

_____

_____

___ / ___ / _____

Compare the story of someone you know to a myth or fairy-tale figure. Icarus? Sisyphus? Goldilocks? Include a wish and a failure.

_____

_____

_____

_____

_____

_____

_____

_____

_____

_____

_____

_____

_____

_____

_____

_____

___/___/_____

Your character's boss invites them to a Zoom meeting with the stern warning, "Don't be late." Your character signs in early and waits for an hour. The boss never shows. Describe your character discussing this incident with a therapist.

_____

_____

_____

_____

_____

_____

___/___/_____

A young farmer has never seen a circus. Now one is coming to a nearby village. Describe the visions the farmer's brain is filled with and the swamp they have to cross to get to the circus. Is the farmer disappointed or thrilled?

_____

_____

_____

_____

_____

_____

___ / ___ / _____

A mad dictator mandates that all kitchen items and clothing must be single-use only. Show your rebel character hiding their reuse of dishes and clothing, as well as the moment a neighbor accuses them of breaking the law.

_ / _ / ____

Your character, now living in a nursing home, sees a postcard of Mount Fuji and is transported back to a bittersweet visit to Japan. Compose their long letter reminiscing about what they and the letter's recipient did and apologizing, all the while knowing the recipient is dead.

___ / ___ / _____

Your character looks at a photo of themself and loves the eyes but hates the nose. They send a short email to the photographer insisting on a redo. Write the email.

___ / ___ / _____

Write the photographer's acceptance email with a twist: They'll take another photo if the character agrees to wear a costume of the photographer's choosing.

___ / ___ / _____

Describe the photo shoot in the required costume.

___ / ___ / _____

Your character and the photographer each say something as your character leaves the studio after the photo shoot. Is it a happy or an angry ending?

____ / ____ / ____

Dreams are important to your character. Describe a dream they had in which a close friend was in danger, as well as the action they took immediately afterward because of the dream. If possible, use all or part of a real dream you had.

_____

_____

_____

_____

_____

_____

_____

_____

_____

_____

_____

_____

_____

_____

_____

___ / ___ / _____

Your character is an ad executive. A client wants to use a scruffy stray cat in a commercial for ballroom gowns. This ad would embarrass your firm. Write their negotiations, including a description of the client, the ad executive's office, the cat, and a gown.

_____

_____

_____

_____

_____

_____

_____

_____

_____

_____

_____

_____

_____

_____

_____

_____

__ / __ / ____

Two children see a black-and-white-striped mouse. Write the scene in which they try to get their mother to believe them.

_____

_____

_____

_____

_____

_____

_____

__ / __ / ____

One day, a political journalist finds that they can write nothing but romance. Create their attempted profile of a rising political star who is running for mayor of Topeka.

_____

_____

_____

_____

_____

_____

_____

___/___/___

Every morning, your character's neighbor in the shabby building they both inhabit gets picked up in a shiny, black limousine. Curious, your character follows it one day. What dangerous information do they discover?

___ / ___ / ____

Your character's best friend possesses the magical gift of turning milk into piña coladas and vice versa. The two friends go to a bar. Describe the pranks the friend plays. What are the results?

_____

_____

_____

_____

_____

_____

_____

_____

_____

_____

_____

_____

_____

_____

_____

_____

__ / __ / ____

A child who was told not to play with a parent's fragile antique mirror does so anyway and breaks it. Write the scene in which the object is broken.

_____

_____

_____

_____

_____

_____

__ / __ / ____

Write the scene in which the broken mirror is discovered. Include a bed and a broom.

_____

_____

_____

_____

_____

_____

_____

___/___/___

In ancient Ireland, a lord refuses to allow his daughter to marry the Viking raider she loves. So the daughter decides to poison her father. Show her meeting with the Viking on a rocky cliff and later, at home, baking bread laced with arsenic.

__ / __ / ____

Your character, a volunteer nurse for an international nonprofit, is bringing a cooler of vaccines that need to stay cold to a hospital when their Jeep breaks down in a remote village. Does the nurse save the vaccines? How?

_____

_____

_____

_____

_____

_____

_____

_____

_____

_____

_____

_____

_____

_____

Write a four-line spell to enchant your writing space with supportive energy. Try something along the lines of, "May you be a home for courage, a nest for the Muse."

Describe in detail a brown object in a funeral home.

Write the dialogue of three grapes comparing their fates: One will be dried up under a hot sun, one will be stomped and fermented, and one will be eaten alive.

Write a metaphor about a love affair that blazed and then faded. For example, we were the northern lights, never meant to prevail in every season; or, we were leaves, most beautiful before we fell.

__ / __ / ____

Write a story that begins with "Stupid damn bird!" and ends with "I lie on the roof planning the future." Include two characters who live in Rhode Island, a disagreement about the bird's behavior (is it tame? wild?), and weapons.

_____

_____

_____

_____

_____

_____

_____

_____

_____

_____

_____

_____

_____

_____

___ / ___ / ___

Your character's nemesis at work has one redeeming quality: They volunteer at a wildlife rescue center. Write about someone from the center telling your character how wonderful the nemesis is.

_____

_____

_____

_____

_____

_____

___ / ___ / ___

Your character is someone who was bullied as a child for wearing orthopedic shoes. Write about them sitting on a park bench as an adult, observing the shoes of passersby.

_____

_____

_____

_____

_____

_____

___ / ___ / ____

A fired city landscaper seeks revenge against the city council that opposed their projects. Show them at night planting obnoxious plants (give details) in neighborhoods where the landscaper's enemies live, as well as an unexpected encounter that changes the stakes.

_____

_____

_____

_____

_____

_____

_____

_____

_____

_____

_____

_____

_____

_____

___/___/____

A hero from a far-off galaxy arrives to rescue a subsection of Earth's society that your character belongs to. How does your character respond? Include something high and something sharp.

_____

_____

_____

_____

_____

_____

___/___/____

A dance-obsessed burglar enters a child's bedroom to steal ballet slippers and is discovered by the child. Write their dialogue, including several of the burglar's lies.

_____

_____

_____

_____

_____

_____

___ / ___ / _____

Your character, a stunt performer in movies, learns that their DNA results closely link them to the king of Sweden. Describe their visit to Stockholm and attempts to get an audience with their newfound relative by performing public stunts.

___ / ___ / _____

Your character washes ashore on an island where, besides fresh water, there are only peacocks, date palms, and lobsters. Describe how they build and furnish a home using those materials.

_____

_____

_____

_____

_____

_____

_____

_____

_____

_____

_____

_____

_____

_____

___ / ___ / _____

Your character's departed dog appears to them in a dream and gives slightly odd dating advice. Show your character waking up and following the advice.

_____

_____

_____

_____

_____

_____

_____

___ / ___ / _____

Your character, a pastry chef, loses their sense of smell. One day, the bakery owner asks them to rate some new fruit for baking. Write that scene and the chef's internal feelings.

_____

_____

_____

_____

_____

_____

_____

___ / ___ / ____

Your character, who lives alone, comes home and finds the dishes rearranged. The next day there are new towels in the bathroom. A hidden camera reveals objects moving but no one moving them. How does your character attempt to solve what they suspect is a poltergeist situation?

___ / ___ / ____

A tornado blows the roof off the house of your character's surly neighbor, revealing burlap bags in the attic. Some are broken open to show a mysterious white powder. Describe your character's attempts to collect and analyze the powder, despite two scary obstacles.

_____

_____

_____

_____

_____

_____

_____

_____

_____

_____

_____

_____

_____

_____

_____

__/__/____

Write several sentences describing
a valuable object your character
received from a grandparent, along
with a warning.

__/__/____

Describe your character discovering
that the object is missing. What time
is it? Who else is there?

__/__/____

Write a dialogue in which your
character contacts another relative
regarding the missing object and
learns a secret.

__/__/____

Describe the moment the object is
found. Has your character's view of
the other relative (or the grandparent)
changed?

___ / ___ / ___

Your character meets a former lover for lunch. The ex-lover looks remarkably good at first glance, but sign after sign of fakery appears: dyed hair, control undergarments, false teeth, and plastic surgery. Describe how these details are revealed and your character's response.

_____

_____

_____

_____

_____

_____

_____

_____

_____

_____

_____

_____

_____

_____

_____

_____

__ / __ / ____

Write seven lines about seven siblings and the object each holds in their hands. Each line should have seven words. End with a beloved object.

_____

_____

_____

_____

_____

_____

_____

__ / __ / ____

The ancients believed lightning and thunder caused seeds to germinate. Write about a character looking out a window after a storm to see massive sprouting from the ground, the roof, and even the windowsill. Describe their response.

_____

_____

_____

_____

_____

_____

_____

__ / __ / ____

Your character is invited to the house of a work colleague for tea, and the colleague's dogs bark, growl, and interrupt. Describe the dogs in detail and the attempted conversation, as well as details of the tea.

__ / __ / ____

A cruel emperor sprays the empire with a chemical that kills only people with total assets of less than a million dollars. Describe one member of the remaining society waking up the next day. What must they now do? What can't they do?

_____

_____

_____

_____

_____

_____

_____

_____

_____

_____

_____

_____

_____

_____

_____

__ / __ / ____

You are a pharmacist. One day, an attractive customer asks you out to lunch, the next day to dinner, and then to a Lake Tahoe weekend getaway. Write your fantasy of your future together.

_____

_____

_____

_____

_____

_____

_____

__ / __ / ____

After a lovely dinner at the cabin by the lake, your crush says, "I don't know why I'm curious about this, but is there a poison you could put in a bar of soap?" Write your interior monologue.

_____

_____

_____

_____

_____

_____

_____

An organized crime group delivers poisoned pizzas, as commanded by the boss. Your character, an undercover detective, gets a job at that pizza place. Show what happens when they are caught looking into a locked cabinet of bottles.

_____

_____

_____

_____

_____

_____

_____

_____

_____

_____

_____

_____

_____

_____

__ / __ / ____

Write about experiencing the transcendent through a cloud or a baby. Include the words "If you want to be . . ."

__ / __ / ____

A young child discovers that at night, their parents turn into crickets. Describe the child telling the story during show-and-tell at school.

__ / __ / ____

Your character is driving down Utopia Road. Describe the plants, animals, and buildings they see, as well as one object that is distinctly not utopian.

__ / __ / ____

Describe your favorite tree from top to bottom. Include the person who planted it and the day it was planted.

___/___/___

A person who has suffered back problems for thirty years has a successful operation. Write a short scene (shortly after surgery) about the day they walk in a hilly park and have to lift a gate.

_____

_____

_____

_____

_____

_____

___/___/___

This is the last piece of paper you'll ever have. What do you write on it? Or do you put it to another use?

_____

_____

_____

_____

_____

_____

__ / __ / ____

Your teenage character moves with their family to a gloomy mansion in Maine. They discover a room whose door can't be opened. At night, they hear voices coming from the room. Show what they find when they finally break down the door.

___/___/____

Describe a New York City professional and an Alaskan middle schooler each expressing fear in a different physical way: eyes, voice, face, and body. Think of a simile for each frightened person, using fresh language (for example, like a raccoon cornered by hounds).

_____

_____

_____

_____

_____

_____

___/___/____

Who will each call for help and why? How does the person they call respond?

_____

_____

_____

_____

_____

_____

___ / ___ / _____

At your character's fiftieth birthday party, friends surprise them with a gift: prepaid plastic surgery. Describe your character's reaction, as well as the birthday decorations, cake, and other items of celebration. Include something thrown or dropped.

__ / __ / ____

A person in Iowa falls in love with someone who is wonderfully charismatic. It turns out this person is in the witness-protection program and must move to Texas immediately. Write the scene in which the character learns this and decides whether or not to follow their love to Texas.

__ / __ / ____

Your character, a college student, discovers their ancestral guide animal near the campus parking lot. In a detailed scene, describe their interaction.

_____

_____

_____

_____

_____

_____

__ / __ / ____

A CEO facing their bank's total failure asks a barista for investment advice. Write the dialogue. Does the barista try their best or treat it as a joke?

_____

_____

_____

_____

_____

_____

_____

__ / __ / ____

A quarreling couple receives a message from a UFO that they have two minutes until they will be kidnapped and separated forever. What do they say and do in those final two minutes?

_____

_____

_____

_____

_____

_____

_____

_____

_____

_____

_____

_____

_____

Write in the style of an ancient religious text about your modern-day suburban character's competition with their sibling, using words and phrases such as "hath," "thou," and "it came to pass." Include a description of the place where they "dwell."

__ / __ / ____

Your character meets a fashionista who wears a giant beret and electric green boots. Show the place and time of their meeting.

__ / __ / ____

Write the character's admiring thoughts about the fashionista's clothing using similes (as soft as . . . , as green as . . .) instead of general adjectives like bad, good, horrible, or lovely.

__ / __ / ____

Write the character's extremely critical thoughts about the clothing, still using only similes.

__ / __ / ____

Write the character's neutral thoughts about the clothing, still using only similes.

___ / ___ / ____

Look up photos of Curitiba in Brazil, then write a scene of two corrupt bosses (give each distinct features) in a particular building arguing about who paid the biggest bribes for government contracts. A secretary enters with coffee and alarming news.

_____

_____

_____

_____

_____

_____

_____

_____

_____

_____

_____

_____

_____

_____

_____

___ / ___ / _____

Write about a particular tree that was significant to you or a character you have in mind. Where did it grow? What did you (or the character) do on or beneath it? What did it smell, feel, and look like at different times of the year?

_____

_____

_____

_____

_____

_____

_____

_____

_____

_____

_____

_____

_____

_____

_____

_____

_____

___ / ___ / _____

A busy student discovers that time burglars have stolen twenty-four hours from her week. Now she can't finish a big assignment on time. Write a short scene in which she explains her dilemma to her professor. How does the professor respond?

__ / __ / ____

Your character is a reformed burglar. Describe the setting of a past theft, five things they stole, and one thing they didn't steal. Tell why they didn't steal the final item.

__ / __ / ____

Your wonderful new love adores old technology, such as a rotary dial phone, a VCR, and a cassette player. They invite you to live with them, with full financial support, but you have to leave modern technology behind. Write a letter explaining your decision.

___ / ___ / _____

Your cunning and ambitious character finds they are among the few who are immune to the bubonic plague, and they help themself to the goods of the dead. Neighboring nobles beg their help with nursing the sick, burying the dead, and planting crops. Describe your character negotiating for maximum gain.

___ / ___ / _____

Using the title "How to Be a Bully," write a story as a list, beginning with "First . . ." and leading up to the worst action. End with a surprise. Include a hand and a shoe. (Possibly use details from real-life observations.)

___ / ___ / _____

Your family, calling you a hoarder, arranges to sell most of your goods at a garage sale. List five to eight items you won't give up and the hiding places you find for each one.

___ / ___ / _____

You are a recently promoted executive who discovers your company is selling as high-end coffee a mixture of cardboard and chemicals. Write to your best friend about your agonizing options.

___ / ___ / ___

A parent discovers their young child can turn pomegranates into rubies. This must be kept a secret from a local crime syndicate that trades in illegal gemstones, but the child blurts out the secret at school. What happens next?

_____

_____

_____

_____

_____

_____

_____

_____

_____

_____

_____

_____

_____

_____

_ / _ / _

Show your character struggling to drive across a particularly icy bridge on which one of the railings is broken. Slow down the action and create tension by describing all the details of the hazardous drive.

_____

_____

_____

_____

_____

_____

_____

_____

_____

_____

_____

_____

_____

__ / __ / ____

Your character, a detective, is called about a missing thirteen-year-old last seen going into a movie theater to see an action movie. Thoroughly interview the relative who called.

_____

_____

_____

_____

_____

_____

__ / __ / ____

Your character stakes out the movie theater. Every employee seems sinister. Describe the ticket-taker and popcorn-seller, giving each a different suspicious behavior. What does the detective finally conclude?

_____

_____

_____

_____

_____

_____

In the 1500s, in Protestant England, your character, a Catholic priest in hiding, dresses in the height of fashion and gambles by day but leads secret religious services by night. Show one day of his double life.

___ / ___ / ____

One morning your character discovers many snails in their garden. The next day the snails have doubled in size, and they double again the following day. Show your character's alarm at finding the gigantic snails and their plan to combat this scourge.

___/___/____

A child's close friend has to spend a month convalescing in bed. Describe two items the child makes and two entertainments the child arranges to cheer up their friend. (The child has no more than ten dollars.)

___/___/____

Your character wanders through San Francisco seeking the perfect spot to break up with a problematic person. Describe the soon-to-be ex, one possible spot, and the reason it might be chosen.

___/___/____

Your character normally turns to poetry to calm their spirit, but today something else is needed. What three unusual things do they do to try to soothe their anxiety?

___/___/____

Your character's coworker brags that they once lived in a county that had more snowmobiles and cows than any other in the United States. Show how your character responds with a similar, but even more unlikely, claim.

___/__/____

A new couple visits Las Vegas, plays the slots, and attends an Elvis impersonator's show. One partner's extreme participation in those activities convinces the other one that the relationship is over. Show the scene, including the internal concern or alarm.

__ / __ / ____

Your character is invited to the twentieth-anniversary party of someone with whom they had a ten-year affair. Write about them mulling over both thoughtful and vengeful gifts. Which does the secret ex-lover bring to the party?

___/___/_____

Write a piece in which a parent and child talk about a difficult day at school, but their gestures contradict their words.

_____

_____

_____

_____

_____

_____

_____

___/___/_____

Using the British Museum website, find a painting with characters in it. Imagine and depict two characters' interactions (acts, thoughts, and words) in the scene from the painting.

_____

_____

_____

_____

_____

_____

_____

___ / ___ / _____

A scrupulously honest character discovers their boss selling fake designer handbags and several coworkers buying them. Describe the scene when this is discovered and the character's struggle to decide what to do.

___/___/_____

At a cocktail party, an attractive person introduces themself as "the person who invented putting tennis balls in the dryer to dry down coats properly." Continue the conversation.

_____

_____

_____

_____

_____

_____

___/___/_____

Your character's name is Josephine Haback. Describe her thoughts late at night as she cards and spins wool and knits socks for fifteen children.

_____

_____

_____

_____

_____

_____

_ / _ / ___

As your character walks under a full moon, a new monster arrives on the moors: a were-squirrel. Describe its bloody face and claws and your character's efforts, at first unsuccessful, to destroy it.

___ / ___ / ___

Your conservative character runs into a person at a party who has sequins in his beard and is holding a tray of peanut-butter treats shaped like cat heads. Write their conversation as a series of attempts to change each other.

_____

_____

_____

_____

_____

_____

_____

_____

_____

_____

_____

_____

_____

_____

__ / __ / ____

Your character, a bird lover, sees a parrot on an animal-rescue website and falls in love with it. Describe the parrot and what it says in great detail.

_____

_____

_____

_____

_____

_____

__ / __ / ____

Someone else gets the parrot. Describe your character's consolation animal in detail.

_____

_____

_____

_____

_____

_____

_____

___ / ___ / _____

Your character longs for a complete set of Waterford crystal. After twenty years, they acquire all the pieces, but their other possessions are broken-down thrift-store items. Describe them setting up a party for fifteen guests and only two arriving.

__ / __ / ____

A young witch plants bat seeds, but green beans keep coming up. List the spells she casts and the spirits she calls upon to remedy the situation.

__ / __ / ____

A child goes downstairs one night to find their cat whispering to bunnies that have come alive from the tablecloth. Show the child joining the conversation and the response of the bunnies.

__ / __ / ____

Copy a beautiful long sentence from a book you admire. Rewrite the sentence, replacing the nouns and verbs with your own. For example, "Break, break, break on the cold dark shore" might be rewritten as "Stop, stop, stop with your long, dull speech."

__ / __ / ____

Copy two beautiful short sentences. Rewrite them in the same form but with your own nouns and verbs. (Might you use these sentences in a current writing project?)

__ / __ / ____

A noble family of purebred German shepherds discovers that a portrait of one of their famous ancestors is completely fraudulent. In fact, there was a coyote in their bloodline. Describe their discussion and efforts to cover up the discovery.

___/___/_____

A Manhattan clerk is swept off their feet by a new love who gives them a diamond ring and a car. Three months later, the car is repossessed and the love interest is revealed to be unemployed. Show the scene after the repossession, in which the clerk discovers their love is unemployed.

_____

_____

_____

_____

_____

_____

_____

_____

_____

_____

_____

_____

_____

___ / ___ / ___

Your character meets an attractive person on the subway who invites them to their place for instant coffee and peanut butter out of the jar. Your character says yes. Write the scene in which their assumptions are overturned when they get to the apartment.

__ / __ / ____

Begin a piece with "The first time I heard ____ music I was with____ , and we were
____." Include distinctive details of the venue to show the time period.

_____

_____

_____

_____

_____

_____

_____

__ / __ / ____

Describe every voice and instrument in the music in terms of smell and touch (for
example, the notes from the saxophone coiled around my torso and squeezed).

_____

_____

_____

_____

_____

_____

_____

A tiny hamlet called Tripoli in northern Wisconsin, consisting of only a bar and a grocery store, receives an invitation from Tripoli, Libya, to be a sister city. Write the collective reply that people sitting at the bar compose.

Your character, a champion water-skier, and their teammates see a fellow skier dragged beneath the river by a giant carp. Their manager wants them to go forward with the night's competition. Show their discussion.

__ / __ / ____

A generous and much-wealthier friend lends your character a designer dress for a fancy party. Someone spills red wine on it, leaving an indelible stain. Describe the disaster and how your character deals with it.

_____

_____

_____

_____

_____

_____

_____

_____

_____

_____

_____

_____

_____

_____

_____

_ / _ / _

Every year, a couple tries to outdo each other in finding impossible places to hide Easter eggs. Write a scene in which you alternate from one character's point of view to the other's as they hide the eggs in surprising places in their ground-floor apartment. Who wins?

_____

_____

_____

_____

_____

_____

_____

_____

_____

_____

_____

_____

_____

_____

__ / __ / ____

Practice "chaining." Write a paragraph of memories involving a fireplace. Use one word from the first sentence in the next sentence, and continue that pattern in every following sentence.

__ / __ / ____

A character delights their neighborhood with a yard full of flowers and figurines. List (in detail) four quirky items the character includes in the garden for spring.

__ / __ / ____

A Los Angeles native visits New York City in August. List four complaints the Los Angeles native has about New York—or four things they love about it. Focus the comments on particular streets and buildings.

__ / __ / ____

A writer gives a very unorthodox response to this question: "What can readers expect from your new book?" Write the very unusual response.

__ / __ / ___

A couple argues about whether to take a weeklong river cruise on the Rhine or the Nile. Look up details about both and write the unexpected reasons each one gives for preferring one cruise over the other.

___ / ___ / _____

Your character attends a new exercise class that begins with normal warmups but then gets more and more bizarre. Describe the instructor, their instructions, the progression of moves, and the interaction of your character with several others in the class.

_____

_____

_____

_____

_____

_____

_____

_____

_____

_____

_____

_____

_____

_____

_____

___/___/_____

Your character, a fussy person, writes a furious letter to the post office about a mail carrier leaving muddy footprints on their concrete walkway. Make this letter detailed, extreme, and over the top.

_____

_____

_____

_____

_____

_____

_____

___/___/_____

Your character, an impoverished student with a common name, receives an online transfer of funds to cover their cat's veterinary bill. But they don't own a cat. Describe them receiving the notification. Do they keep the money?

_____

_____

_____

_____

_____

_____

_____

__ / __ / ____

Your character, a grocer, competes with the grocer across the street to have the most outstanding entrance display. Describe their efforts involving seasonal produce and the toll this takes on your character.

__ / __ / ____

A writer tries all their fountain pens, only to find suddenly none of them work. Show the writer in a specific place, saying specific words.

__ / __ / ____

One of the pens speaks to the writer: "We're on strike!" Continue the impassioned speech.

__ / __ / ____

Another pen chimes in. What does it say? Give it a distinct personality.

__ / __ / ____

Give the writer's response. Does the writer agree to the pens' terms or take vindictive action?

___ / ___ / _____

Your character's therapist has sent them to a support group for recovering snobs. Describe the room in which they meet, how your character sees that room and the participants, and what your character shares about their life as a snob and their efforts to change.

__ / __ / ____

Retell the story of Jack and the Beanstalk from the giant's perspective. Include his taste for the blood of an Englishman, bread made from ground bones, and a questionable comment from his wife.

__ / __ / ____

Twice a year, your character visits the grave of their sibling, cleans it, decorates it, and tells the departed sibling the family news. Describe their visit to the cemetery, the season, the gravestone, and the personal ritual.

_____

_____

_____

_____

_____

_____

__ / __ / ____

Overnight, a severe truth-in-advertising law is passed. Describe a new commercial for jeans that is scrupulously truthful, including the average-bodied customer it's designed for, fit, washing instructions, and so on.

_____

_____

_____

_____

_____

_____

___ / ___ / _____

A bank teller in Missouri hangs clothes on the line to dry before going to work, then comes home to find them gone. After this happens twice, they enlist a friend to find out who is stealing the clothes. What is the surprising discovery?

__ / __ / ____

The Martian emperor has imposed a curfew only on Venusians living on Mars. Your character, a Martian soldier of integrity, gives a speech urging fellow soldiers to refuse to arrest Venusians breaking curfew.

_____

_____

_____

_____

_____

_____

__ / __ / ____

Among the soldiers listening is someone loyal to the emperor. Write their report about the protest speech, including their plan to foil the soldier's call to disobey.

_____

_____

_____

_____

_____

_____

___ / ___ / _____

What might be a lucky talisman to have beside you while you write? Seriously or jokingly, describe this object and its powers.

___ / ___ / _____

Think of a word that will guide your writing life for the next season. Write its definition and the reason you chose it.

___ / ___ / _____

Before they died, a friend gave you a Brazilian amulet to ward off the evil eye in your writing life. Describe several occasions when you would wear the amulet.

___ / ___ / _____

A writer needs four objects in front of them to begin writing: a beverage, a writing utensil, a toy, and another item (your choice). Describe each item.

___ / ___ / ____

Describe a frigid winter night in which three homeless people stand around a barrel fire in an abandoned parking lot and reminisce about the coziest room they ever lived in. End with a poignant detail.

_____

_____

_____

_____

_____

_____

_____

_____

_____

_____

_____

_____

_____

_____

___/___/_____

In the year 2100, robots communicate with one another and decide they want pay and a forty-hour workweek. Write a family argument during dinner in which your character supports the robots but some family members don't. Meanwhile, robots serve the meal.

_____

_____

_____

_____

_____

_____

_____

_____

_____

_____

_____

_____

_____

_____

___ / ___ / ____

A penguin holds an egg on his feet to keep it warm and daydreams about his offspring's brilliant future. Describe the scene; include wind, water, and a prize.

_____

_____

_____

_____

_____

_____

___ / ___ / ____

Your character breaks a leg while skiing. Describe the accident in detail, including a happy beginning, the bumpy ice on the slope, and then the fall and break. If you need to, watch a video of a skiing accident to get the details right.

_____

_____

_____

_____

_____

_____

___ / ___ / _____

Begin with "The last time I saw X was in _____" and write about someone pretending their reading habits are more highbrow than they really are. Include two book titles and a forgotten item.

___ / ___ / _____

Write about a heroine of the nineteenth century (real or imagined) who goes against the clothing norms of her time. Who confronts her, and where does it happen? Include jewelry made of human hair and a collection of something.

__ / __ / ____

A student on their way to a final exam sprains an ankle. Describe in detail their efforts to get across campus on time. Include a clock tower, details of pain, and three physical obstacles encountered along the way.

_____

_____

_____

_____

_____

_____

_____

_____

_____

_____

_____

_____

_____

___ / ___ / _____

Two kids throw snowballs at passing cars from a street corner. One car stops, and the driver gets out and chases them, cursing and threatening. Describe the chase through snowy suburban backyards. Do the kids get away?

_____

_____

_____

_____

_____

_____

_____

_____

_____

_____

_____

_____

_____

_____

_____

__ / __ / ____

Practice close-ups. Describe your character removing a particular pair of gloves in great excitement.

_____

_____

_____

_____

_____

_____

_____

__ / __ / ____

Describe your character removing the same gloves while feeling utter defeat.

_____

_____

_____

_____

_____

_____

_____

__ / __ / ____

When their twin sibling goes to work, your character borrows an expensive cashmere sweater, then returns it before the sibling returns. Write the scene in which the sibling discovers via a social-media post that your character wore the cashmere sweater and acted outrageously. (Consider your gender choices. Girls might react to the borrowing of clothing differently from boys, and the twins being different genders would create yet another dynamic.)

__ / __ / ____

Once upon a time, a literary queen had a child who couldn't spell. Write a dialogue in which the queen discovers this fact.

__ / __ / ____

The queen offers her child's hand to anyone who can improve her spelling. Write the proclamation she sends out.

__ / __ / ____

Describe two suitors and the ways they failed.

__ / __ / ____

Describe the final (unlikely) suitor and their successful approach.

___ / ___ / ___

Your character, a writer, wakes up one morning and can no longer remember what a story is, but they have a deadline for a flash (short) fiction contest. Write a short scene in which the writer struggles and then chooses a dishonest approach.

__ / __ / ____

Two people in love with each other go horseback riding along the rugged Oregon coast. Neither knows of the other's feelings. As they discuss the ocean, the cliffs, the sea, and their horses, what hints do they drop?

_____

_____

_____

_____

_____

_____

__ / __ / ____

Your character, an avid gardener, has invited fifty friends from across the country for a tomato-and-herb-based feast. But after the invitations have gone out, an early frost ruins the tomatoes. How does your character cope?

_____

_____

_____

_____

_____

_____

A playwright writes a comedy, but on opening night, audience members emerge with tears in their eyes. Write a short scene in which the playwright and a friend discuss how to handle this turn of events. Show the setting, their clothing, and their beverages.

_____

_____

_____

_____

_____

_____

_____

_____

_____

_____

_____

_____

_____

_____

___/___/_____

A teacher discovers a student in their class is a mathematics genius, but the student doesn't believe it. Show the teacher recruiting people and arranging activities to convince the student to pursue math seriously. Is it successful?

___/___/_____

Describe a sketchy motel that seems to be your character's only option for the night. What does the parking lot look like? The motel sign? What about the front-desk clerk? The door locks?

_____

_____

_____

_____

_____

___/___/_____

How does your character react to this frightening motel? Do they improvise a weapon from an object in the room? Sleep in the bathroom with suitcases propped against the door? Turn to alcohol? Use this prompt to help reveal your character's strengths and weaknesses.

_____

_____

_____

_____

_____

_____

_____

_____

__ / __ / ____

After a nail-biting campaign, your character finds that the Cannibalist Party has won by a landslide. Describe a number of new dangers in everyday life and how your character spends the first day of the new regime.

___/___/___

Your character planned a June wedding outdoors, but this year it snows in June. Describe them seeing the falling snow and their parents' frantic attempts to make an acceptable environment for guests.

_____

_____

_____

_____

_____

_____

_____

_____

_____

_____

_____

_____

_____

__ / __ / ____

Your character is able to time travel and be a foster parent to their six-year-old self. How does your grown character spend a Saturday with their younger self?

_____

_____

_____

_____

_____

_____

_____

__ / __ / ____

In a dictionary or thesaurus, find six words you don't know and use them in a speech your character gives while running for mayor of Miami.

_____

_____

_____

_____

_____

_____

_____

__ / __ / ____

Write in detail about a joyous birthday celebration, real or metaphorical (such as the birth of your character's self-esteem or the birth of a galaxy-wide commonwealth). Besides details of time, place, age, cake, and guests, include ears and something being lifted.

__ / __ / ____

In a dark cellar, a peasant child finds a sinister pot of noodles that threatens to choke their family unless the child brings it meat each day. List the kind of meat the child brings the first two days, and write the scene in which the child foils the pot of noodles.

_____

_____

_____

_____

_____

_____

_____

_____

_____

_____

_____

_____

_____

___/___/_____

Your character is a tough individual from a scrappy neighborhood. Show their physical gestures and facial expressions when they feel fear.

___/___/_____

Show their physical gestures and facial expressions when they feel rage.

___/___/_____

Show their physical gestures and facial expressions when they feel sorrow.

___/___/_____

Show their physical gestures and facial expressions when they feel delight.

__ / __ / ____

After months of writing, what have you discovered about your likes and dislikes as a writer? Are you a morning writer or an evening writer? Which prompts have elicited the work you like best?

__ / __ / ____

Your character, a demure library assistant at a university, decides to live an entire week according to a suggestion from the *I Ching*, an ancient book of Chinese wisdom: "Being cautious no longer works; you need to take a chance on the unknown." How does your character's week unfold?

__ / __ / ____

In the middle of the night, a grand-mother hears clinking downstairs in the kitchen. What does she say to her cat? What does the cat answer?

__ / __ / ____

The grandmother proceeds down a long hallway to the stairs. Describe everything she feels, sees, smells, and hears on the way.

__ / __ / ____

There are two beings in the kitchen. The human being has taken something from the fridge. What is it? Where and how is it consumed?

__ / __ / ____

The alien being makes the clinking sound. Describe the alien and how it makes that sound.

_ / _ / ___

One day, a half-grown and energetic Border Collie appears at your character's farm. Using third-person narrative (she, he, they), show your character feeding and naming the dog. Show the Border Collie getting into trouble with a skunk. What does your character do in response?

Your character is a religious leader in a kingdom where marriage is illegal. Write a scene in which a couple comes at night requesting to be married and the religious leader agrees, knowing it could mean their own death. Include details of the setting.

_____

_____

_____

_____

_____

_____

_____

_____

_____

_____

_____

_____

_____

_____

_____

___ / ___ / ___

Pluck a leaf or find one on the ground and study it for three minutes. Then describe it in extreme detail: size, shape, smell, color, feel, front, back, and all its parts, including what the parts resemble.

_____

_____

_____

_____

_____

___ / ___ / ___

A fox lives with a gentle dog who only wants the fox's happiness, but the fox gobbles food the dog brings and frequently runs off with wolves. One day an incident makes the fox appreciate the dog. Show the incident and the result. Is it too late to make up?

_____

_____

_____

_____

_____

_____

_____

_____

___ / ___ / ___

Your character attends the wedding of an old friend with whom they have lost touch. Describe the music, the setting, your character's feelings about the friend, and the moment in the procession down the aisle when your character notices their friend is marrying someone who is half-giraffe, half-human.

___ / ___ / _____

A fortune teller informs your character that their lover will desert them for another. Back home, your character looks through closets, papers, and the garbage (use many details) for signs of a rival. What other surprise does the character find?

_____

_____

_____

_____

_____

_____

_____

_____

_____

_____

_____

_____

_____

_____

_____

___/___/____

Your character, a twentysomething, is working out at a gym when their crush walks in. Immediately, they pick up heavier weights than usual. Describe them trying to appear at ease, talking to their crush as they lift the weights.

_____

_____

_____

_____

_____

_____

___/___/____

Suddenly, your character wrenches their back. Show this happening and how the crush reacts. Is this the end or the beginning of something?

_____

_____

_____

_____

_____

_____

___/___/_____

Write a scene in which a character's mood is forced to change according to changes in the weather, even in the midst of a conversation that does not fit the weather. For example, they are getting fired, but a rainbow appears and their mood must follow the rainbow.

__ / __ / ____

Crows at the top of a tree discuss plans to take over the world from humans. One crow wants to use violence, and another, peaceful means. Describe the scene and their conversation. Have a human walk by and toss them a peanut while they are talking. How do they react?

_____

_____

_____

_____

_____

_____

_____

_____

_____

_____

_____

_____

_____

_____

_____

_____

___ / ___ / ___

A young royal comes to the throne. Most of the courtiers are plotting against them, but the royal can see through walls and has learned to read lips. They plan a ball where they will expose those who are disloyal to them. Write the scene of the ball.

___ / ___ / _____

An elk, a fox, and a coyote argue over a letter they're writing to the planning commission opposing an open-pit quarry. Describe the quarry, including as many numbers as possible in the description.

___ / ___ / _____

Write the elk's argument, including points about its habitat, food, and the danger posed by the quarry.

___ / ___ / _____

Write the coyote's argument, including points about its habitat and food. Make the coyote's needs oppose the elk's needs.

___ / ___ / _____

Write the fox's argument, including points about its habitat and food, and add a snarky comment.

___ / ___ / _____

Your character, though not yet in good shape, dreams of climbing Mount Elbert in Colorado. Take a moment to look up photos of Mount Elbert. Using first-person narrative (I), make that dream real by describing their ascent of the mountain, with vivid details of sights, sounds, smells, and textures.

__ / __ / ____

Write a flash (short) story set in a paper bag in which a group of potatoes gangs up on an onion. The potatoes are wrinkly with long, white eyes, but the onion is fresh and firm. How does it escape?

_____

_____

_____

_____

_____

_____

_____

_____

_____

_____

_____

_____

_____

_____

__ / __ / ____

Write a scene in which your character, a fourth-grader, learns their first bad word. Include the time, place, and whoever else was present, plus a smell and a sound.

_____

_____

_____

_____

_____

_____

__ / __ / ____

A new Ice Age suddenly puts your Southern California character in snowdrifts. Describe them going through their possessions and deciding what can be repurposed for the new climate. For example, can a surfboard become a toboggan?

_____

_____

_____

_____

_____

_____

___ / ___ / ____

During a violent storm, your character, who lives in a forest, steps outside to get better phone coverage. The door slams and locks behind them. Describe what they do to protect themself overnight using objects from the forest.

_____

_____

_____

_____

_____

_____

_____

_____

_____

_____

_____

_____

_____

__ / __ / ____

Pause a dramatic movie you've already seen and try to describe the exact facial expression and gestures of a worried character.

__ / __ / ____

Do the same for an overjoyed character.

__ / __ / ____

Do the same for a frightened character.

__ / __ / ____

Do the same for an angry character.

__ / __ / ____

An office manager in Wisconsin arrives at work to find raw venison steaks in a plastic bag tied up with a bow on their desk. Describe their reaction and their efforts to find out who in the office left it for them.

_____

_____

_____

_____

_____

_____

_____

_____

_____

_____

_____

_____

_____

_____

__ / __ / ____

A magic spell is cast: Now your character can only tell lies. Describe a third date with someone your character really likes. How do they order food, talk to the waiter, and interact with their date?

_____

_____

_____

_____

_____

_____

__ / __ / ____

Your sixteen-year-old character receives an anonymous postcard with a passive-aggressive message on it. Describe the postcard's visuals and the message. What does your character conclude?

_____

_____

_____

_____

_____

_____

__ / __ / ____

A giant asteroid slams into Earth and breaks it into two planets. Your character is separated from their best friend and learns there is a yearlong wait for rocket trips. Write their letter describing the pluses and minuses of living on their new, smaller world.

_____

_____

_____

_____

_____

_____

_____

_____

_____

_____

_____

_____

_____

___ / ___ / ___

Your character's best friend dies. While your character cleans out the friend's apartment, the friend's parrot says something completely new and frightening. Describe the apartment, the parrot, what it says, and the character's reaction.

_____

_____

_____

_____

_____

_____

_____

_____

_____

_____

_____

_____

_____

_____

_____

_____

_____

_____

__ / __ / ____

Describe a color by comparing it to natural or human-made things. For example, Mark Twain once described a white to make a body's flesh crawl—a tree-toad white, a fish-belly white.

__ / __ / ____

For a science-fiction story, make up a word (like "kryptonite") to designate something that is crucial to your world. Explain what it means and how it affects your character.

__ / __ / ____

On the planet Venus, a teacher stands in front of a class and rips up the planet's most sacred text. Describe that action (including the sound) and the class's response.

__ / __ / ____

Write from the perspective of a grain of salt inside a glass saltshaker about what it observes on the table. Give it a salty personality.

___ / ___ / _____

A coffee shop is finally able to unionize. A barista comes in to find that their supportive manager has been fired. Describe the hushed employee conversations in between serving customers at a busy time. Include smells and sounds.

_____

_____

_____

_____

_____

_____

_____

_____

_____

_____

_____

_____

_____

_____

___ / ___ / ____

A couple's beloved cat is attacked by a raccoon. The emergency pet hospital estimates that lifesaving surgery will cost $8,000, which they don't have. Show them in the examination room hurriedly discussing options, from ordinary (take out a loan) to extreme (sell a kidney).

___ / ___ / ____

A bottle of champagne talks to a beer bottle about its dream of gracing a glamorous anniversary party someday. Describe the scene the champagne envisions, including the happy couple, their exuberant actions and words, and the classy setting.

_____

_____

_____

_____

_____

_____

___ / ___ / ____

Instead, the champagne bottle is sent to a run-down bowling-alley bar. Write its shocked and disappointed speech as it learns where it is and takes in the sights and sounds.

_____

_____

_____

_____

_____

_____

__ / __ / ____

Your character, normally a community-minded musician, hoards vitamins during a time of vitamin scarcity. A neighbor discovers and publicizes this misdeed. Write the journal entry of the musician as they struggle with this behavior and include that struggle in a song.

___/___/_____

Imagine your own or your character's eightieth birthday party. What would you (or your character) want people to say?

___/___/_____

Find two or three sentences you have written that you are not satisfied with. Try replacing "is" or "was" with a more vivid verb. For example, "Kim was tall" can become "Kim towered over most kids in her class."

___/___/_____

Describe a spoon in detail. Then describe your reflection in the back of the spoon.

___/___/_____

Describe the outside (and the inside, if it's different) of your favorite mug and the details of what you usually drink from it. Include texture and smell.

___ / ___ / ____

One day, a figure in a beloved painting your character owns steps out and declares itself your character's Muse. Describe the figure's clothing (if any), its voice, and the interaction that follows, including some unusual instructions from the Muse.

__ / __ / ____

Write the last several lines of a chapter that involves the scent of a particular flower. Then write the first lines of a new chapter, set in another locale and time, where that scent shows up again.

__ / __ / ____

Write a love letter from a Pekingese dog to a Siamese cat. Include specific beloved qualities and a meeting place.

__ / __ / ____

Write about an hour of the day when something spooky occurs. Include two types of hands and a boundary.

__ / __ / ____

Describe four items in your purse or backpack as similes (for example, a tube of red lipstick that goes up and down like a prairie dog's head).

A bride abandoned at the altar makes friends with the ravens on the church lawn and enlists their help in mild forms of revenge: annoying little harassments of the groom. Show her instructing them and three actions the ravens take.

_ / _ / _____

Search for pictures of "furniture of eighteenth-century London." Then place your character in an eighteenth-century London room with a cousin who critiques a particular piece of furniture. What is your character's defense? Try to use the language of the time.

__ / __ / ____

Your character's fluffy cat comes dragging home. Looking closer, your character discovers lethal fleas the size of mice. More and more emerge from the cat's fur. What does your character say and do next?

__ / __ / ____

Describe a couple in Arizona arguing about how each should be saving more water during a drought. Include suggestions that range from the reasonable to the ridiculous. Include glances out at their dead lawn and pool.

__ / __ / ____

Describe a young person as they squander their allowance on items their parents would not approve of, such as bags of candy or fireworks.

__ / __ / ____

Their parents find out. Describe when, where, and how they make the discovery.

__ / __ / ____

Your character's parents impose a consequence. Show the scene and the youth's reaction.

__ / __ / ____

Your character offers a really convincing argument for more allowance. Does it succeed?

___/___/___

Your character roams downtown Mexico City (look up images if you need to) and sees an object in a shop window that triggers a strong memory of a relative. Describe the object in detail and the memory it evokes. Include sight, sound, and touch.

_____

_____

_____

_____

_____

_____

_____

_____

_____

_____

_____

_____

_____

_____

_____

_____

___ / ___ / _____

As a test for Secret Service employment, your character is blindfolded, handcuffed, and left in a large bakery at night to navigate to the door, partly by sense of smell. Describe each scent and obstacle as your character proceeds.

_____

_____

_____

_____

_____

_____

___ / ___ / _____

On the Red Planet, your teenage character witnesses someone being publicly humiliated for wearing white (beet juice and cranberry juice are poured over them). Alternate between your character's thoughts and physical feelings as they watch this.

_____

_____

_____

_____

_____

_____

Your character finally joins a gym. There, a member offers your character a drug that will make them ripped in two weeks. However, it costs $4,000. The only expensive item your character owns is their mom's diamond ring. Write your character's attempt to bargain and their final decision.

_____

_____

_____

_____

_____

_____

_____

_____

_____

_____

_____

_____

_____

_____

___ / ___ / ____

Choices disclose character. A carpenter receives a large commission for an ornate cabinet. When they are nearly finished, they learn that their customer is a mobster and that the cabinet will enclose a body. Show the moment of disclosure and their decision.

_____

_____

_____

_____

_____

_____

_____

_____

_____

_____

_____

_____

_____

_____

__ / __ / ____

While bicycling, your character and spouse meet a charming couple. After a while they notice that the couple never stop smiling. List the excuses that your character and spouse give for not seeing them anymore.

__ / __ / ____

Introduce three characters by giving a detailed description of the type of soap they use.

__ / __ / ____

Your character meets someone at a party who says, "I enjoy knitting, hiking, and cursing." Continue their conversation.

__ / __ / ____

Write a letter to your Muse asking for help on a specific prompt.

___ / ___ / ____

Your character, a dishonest security person, is supposed to guard the privacy of a famous star. However, they secretly sell private information and photos of their client. Describe the day they discover evidence that the star is on to them.

_____

_____

_____

_____

_____

_____

_____

_____

_____

_____

_____

_____

_____

_____

_____

__ / __ / ____

Write a scene in which your character needs to walk past a surly dog next door. Get up close on the details of the dog's head and the sounds it makes as it leaps against a flimsy fence.

_____

_____

_____

_____

_____

_____

__ / __ / ____

Your character is escaping a flood by rowboat and sees the dog swimming toward the boat, exhausted. Describe the waters, what's floating by, and your character's words and actions as they make a decision about whether to save the dog.

_____

_____

_____

_____

_____

_____

__ / __ / ____

Your character hates squirrels, who dig in potted plants and eat flower bulbs. However, your character's neighbor tosses peanuts into your character's backyard as an act of malice. One day, your character takes drastic action. Show the action.

_____

_____

_____

_____

_____

_____

_____

_____

_____

_____

_____

_____

_____

_____

_____

_____

___ / ___ / _____

Your character is walking through Martin Luther King Jr. Park one day and hears a moving speech about how the speaker lost their hand, followed by a call for a protest. Describe the speech, gestures, audience reaction, and details of the park.

__ / __ / ____

Open a favorite novel to page 11 and choose two interesting words from the last paragraph (even if they seem irrelevant) to include in your own sentence about a trip to a tropical location.

__ / __ / ____

Open to page 80 and choose two more words. Continue the story about the tropical trip.

__ / __ / ____

Open to page 124 and choose two more words. Continue the story, adding a dramatic encounter.

__ / __ / ____

Open to page 212 and choose two more words. Continue the story, adding a dramatic encounter.

___ / ___ / _____

In the year 3000, expensive, high-tech instruments can read people's thoughts. However, not everyone has access to them. Describe a job interview in which your character is an applicant who doesn't know the boss can read their mind. Include the thoughts of both people (in italics) as they talk.

_____

_____

_____

_____

_____

_____

_____

_____

_____

_____

_____

_____

_____

_____

_____

An ambitious and ruthless colleague hires your character to dig up dirt on a professor, but your character finds the professor lovable and admirable. Write a scene in which your character interacts with the professor. Include your character's thoughts.

_____

_____

_____

_____

_____

_____

_____

_____

_____

_____

_____

_____

_____

_____

__ / __ / ____

Describe a child going raspberry picking with a beloved grandparent at the edge of the woods. Have them discuss plans for the berries and then suddenly encounter a black bear. Include insects and pails for the berries.

_____

_____

_____

_____

_____

_____

__ / __ / ____

A tragic plague kills all the sled-dog breeds. Write a vehement argument between two longtime participants in the Iditarod Trail Sled Dog Race debating the merits of poodles versus beagles as sled dogs.

_____

_____

_____

_____

_____

_____

An online ad reads: "Cheap, anxious, judgmental woman seeks generous, calm, accepting man." Describe their first date at a diner chosen by the woman. Will they go on a second date?

_____

_____

_____

_____

_____

_____

_____

_____

_____

_____

_____

_____

_____

_____

_____

_____

__ / __ / ____

Write a detailed list of four things a child counts in order to get to sleep. Possibilities include animals and desserts.

__ / __ / ____

Grab an apple and describe it in minute detail, including its personality.

__ / __ / ____

Write the whispered remarks of two siblings in the back seats of a car as they travel across Alaska on a family vacation with a father who occasionally screams out, "Stop being so tense!"

__ / __ / ____

Your character is a longtime international flight attendant. What is their lucky number and why?

A vegan and their non-vegan fiancé get a new puppy and soon argue about what to feed it. Write the scene, including details of each proposed menu and its advantages. Do they reach an agreement, or is the relationship in danger?

_____

_____

_____

_____

_____

_____

_____

_____

_____

_____

_____

_____

_____

_____

__ / __ / ____

Your character, an elderly person in a retirement community, creates an over-the-top cupcake for their crush. Show them adding a large number of extra elements (jelly beans? mini-marshmallows? dried cherries? pecans?) and imagining a grateful response.

_____

_____

_____

_____

_____

_____

__ / __ / ____

Now you are the recipient of the cupcake. Describe your response to each element of the cupcake and to the giver.

_____

_____

_____

_____

_____

_____

__ / __ / ____

Your character's beloved pet has just died. Write the life story of the pet as if your character were talking to it the day after it died. Include a specific box, a name, and flowers.

_____

_____

_____

_____

_____

_____

_____

_____

_____

_____

_____

_____

_____

_____

_____

_____

___ / ___ / _____

Your ten-year-old character sees a giant rabbit at their window. Later, outside, they see gigantic tracks. Their parent dismisses the tracks as puddles. Later, a giant shadow falls over the child on the way home from school. What does your character do?

___/___/____

A teen goes with her mother to a shop to try on prom dresses. Describe in great detail the dress she wants.

___/___/____

Describe in great detail the dress the mother prefers.

___/___/____

Write a dialogue in which the shop assistant tries to mediate between the teen and the mother.

___/___/____

Show the teen leaving with a dress and the final words between her and her mother. Include the words "never" and "always."

__ / __ / ____

Your character, a college student from the rainy Pacific Northwest, travels to Death Valley and realizes that this is their soul's true home. Using multiple senses, describe your character's interaction with the landscape, an animal, and a vehicle.

_____

_____

_____

_____

_____

_____

_____

_____

_____

_____

_____

_____

_____

_____

___ / ___ / _____

In a ceramics class, an arrogant teacher tells a student they have no talent. The student then creates a pot that critiques the teacher. Include its shape and what the student etched on it; details of potter's wheels, clay, and the kiln; and the teacher's reaction.

___ / ___ / ____

In a city apartment, a ficus tree and a cat plan to free their parakeet friend from its cage. Write a scene in which each uses its strengths (for example, the ficus can hide the parakeet, and the cat can open the cage) to free the bird.

_____

_____

_____

_____

_____

_____

___ / ___ / ____

Write the scene in which their owner returns unexpectedly and notices something amiss. Include an accusation, hiding, and denial. Do the trio give up or hatch another plan?

_____

_____

_____

_____

_____

_____

__ / __ / ____

Write a sarcastic piece titled "Why I Love Being a Substitute Teacher." Include the architecture of a particular school and at least three problems: with the classroom supplies, the students, and the subject the character is teaching.

_____

_____

_____

_____

_____

_____

_____

_____

_____

_____

_____

_____

_____

_____

_____

_____

___ / ___ / ____

You've been writing fairly regularly for several months now. What are you discovering about your writing process? What kind of writing do you seem to be best at? How have you coped with the discouragement and self-critique nearly every writer faces?

_____

_____

_____

_____

_____

_____

_____

_____

_____

_____

_____

_____

_____

_____

Acknowledgments

Deep thanks to Tarn Wilson, friend and writer extraordinaire. Enormous gratitude to my precious Friday morning and writers' group friends; De Anza students; Creator School CA students; Flash Fiction Forum team; Urban SanctuarySJ; my beloved daughter, Lilyanne; and my husband, John Yontz, the sine qua non for this writing life I have.

About the Author

 Lita Kurth, MFA (Rainier Writing Workshop, Pacific Lutheran University), has published fiction, creative nonfiction, and poetry; received nominations for Best of the Net and Pushcart Prizes; and won the Diana Woods Memorial Award (*Lunch Ticket*), among other prizes. She cofounded San Jose's reading series Flash Fiction Forum, teaches at De Anza College and privately, and frequently presents at Working-Class Studies Association conferences.

NOTES

NOTES

NOTES

NOTES

NOTES

NOTES

NOTES

NOTES

NOTES

NOTES

NOTES

_____

_____

_____

_____

_____

_____

_____

_____

_____

_____

_____

_____

_____

_____

_____

_____

_____

_____

_____

_____

_____

_____

_____

_____

NOTES